CONSCIOUS KIDS SERIES BOOK ONE

Vegan for the Animals

First Edition

Created by

M. FAIRLAMB & C. MICHELLE

Copyright © Michael Fairlamb 2018

Published in 2018 by Elevating Peace

The books in the Conscious Kids Series are dedicated to those who wish to care for our planet and all who live on it.

Important Information about the Conscious Kids Series

The Conscious Kids Series is intended to be a teaching tool for children of all ages who are unfamiliar with veganism and its implications on animals, our health and the environment. The various topics were written with children of all ages in mind which means certain aspects are intentionally left out or not expanded upon too deeply. The goal with this series is to reveal enough about the subjects to give a solid foundation of understanding which can be built upon over time, without going into so much detail that children are left feeling overwhelmed.

The Conscious Kids Series covers the negative impacts of animal agriculture and the consumption of animal products on animals, the environment and our bodies. Inevitably these topics can be unpleasant but are necessary to convey if we wish for our children to develop an understanding of them. We recommend that parents and caregivers skim over the books to make sure they are comfortable with the content the children in their care will be learning.

We truly hope you find this series to be a valuable teaching tool. If you have any questions, comments or suggestions for the series we would be happy to hear from you. We can be reached at consciouskidsseries@gmail.com.

Please note: The information contained in this series is not meant to be taken as medical or professional advice. Please seek the advice of a medical or nutrition professional before making any decisions on dietary intake.

Table of Contents

The Farming Industry	Page 4
Factory Farming	Page 6
The Dairy Industry	Page 8
The Veal Industry	Page 11
The Beef Industry	Page 12
The Pork Industry	Page 14
The Poultry Industry	Page 18
The Egg Industry	Page 20
The Fishing Industry	Page 22
The Humane Myth	Page 26
Animals used for Entertainment	Page 28
The Textile Industry	Page 30
Animals as Pets	Page 32
Animal Testing	Page 34
Choosing Compassion	Page 36

VEGAN FOR THE ANIMALS

Although there are many good things which come from people choosing a **vegan** lifestyle, those who benefit most from this choice are without a doubt the animals. To live a vegan lifestyle means to do what is possible and reasonable to prevent harm to animals. The choice to be vegan comes from a place of respect for animals and a belief that they are **sentient beings** who deserve to carry out their lives naturally and without human interference. This book is here to help you understand the many ways animals suffer at the hands of humans, and just how much of a difference each person makes by choosing to live a vegan lifestyle.

Millions of people all around the world choose to live compassionate lifestyles by being vegan. More and more people each day are choosing to become vegan after learning about how their life choices can affect the wellbeing of animals.

Animals in Nature

Animals are intelligent and affectionate beings. They care for and protect their families and others they bond with. They naturally love to **forage** for food, build nests, keep themselves clean, play, cuddle, and seek shelter from predators and bad weather. The bottom line is - animals exist for their own reasons separate from humans.

Pigs in their natural environment.

Removed From Nature

Unfortunately humans have taken advantage of their ability to control animals in order to eat certain foods, be entertained, or to possess products which are either tested on animals or made using their skin or fur. For many animals, their natural **instincts** are impossible to carry out, and sadly they endure their lives in the most unnatural and scary conditions.

ANIMAL FARMING INDUSTRIES

Each year tens of billions of animals around the world endure terrible circumstances and are eventually killed in order for farming industries to produce food to sell to consumers. Farms are businesses and businesses exist to make money. Unfortunately enough people continue to pay money for these products which makes it possible for farms to stay in business. There are many types of animal farming that occur, but not all of them will be discussed here. The most common ones will be explored in this book including: dairy, cattle, pig, chicken, turkey, egg and fish farming.

Artificial Reproduction

In order for farms to keep their production high they often force the animals to reproduce by **artificial insemination** rather than allowing them to reproduce as they would naturally. This involves humans doing things to the animals which are extremely unnatural, uncomfortable and painful. Most animals used for reproducing are forced to become pregnant multiple times before they are sent to slaughter.

Insemination cage.

Slaughter

Slaughter is the word used to describe the killing of animals in order to use their bodies for the purpose of creating products. There are many ways animals are slaughtered in the farming industry. This book is intended for children of all ages, so the details of slaughtering methods will not be discussed as they can be quite upsetting.

Transport

When animals reach the desired size or age, they are transported to where they will be slaughtered. They are loaded onto trailers with so many animals crammed together that they are often unable to turn around or move much at all. These trailers are open to the outside air, so the animals are exposed to all weather conditions including extreme heat, below freezing temperatures, rain, snow and storms. They spend up to several days in the trucks with no food or water forced to endure harsh weather conditions, loud busy roads, and to stand in their own waste until they finally arrive at the slaughterhouse.

FACTORY FARMING

When people think of animals on farms, most imagine them roaming in open fields and doing whatever they want free from any harsh conditions. Unfortunately this is not the case for most farmed animals. Factory farming is a type of farming that seeks to produce a high amount of products in a very short amount of time while keeping costs to a minimum for the farming company. This is the way most farming is now done.

In factory farms animals are confined to such small spaces they are often unable to sit down or turn around – either because they are crammed inside spaces with too many other animals or because they are in extremely small cages.

Life in a Factory Farm

Pigs inside of a factory farm.

Animals in factory farms suffer through stressful and dirty circumstances throughout their short lives. They have no choice but to stand in their own waste because they are unable to get away from it. They also have no choice but to breathe in the strong fumes from their waste which builds up inside due to poor ventilation. This causes breathing difficulty and diseases of the lungs. They experience painful procedures with no pain medication, and many of the animals end up with diseases or infections which cause them pain and oftentimes death.

Food Products

The majority of food items for sale today that contain animal products are a result of factory farming. This means almost all of the items in grocery stores or restaurants containing meat, eggs or dairy are a result of factory farming and its especially cruel practices.

Living Compassionately

As more people choose to make their food choices based on compassion for animals, less animals are having to endure conditions of factory farms or any farms at all.

THE DAIRY INDUSTRY

Dairy is the word used to describe milk that is produced by cows. In addition to dairy being sold by itself as milk, it is also used to make many food products including cheese, butter and ice cream among many others. Dairy farming is the farming process animals go through which causes them to produce milk so it can be taken from their bodies. Most dairy products available for purchase are obtained from cows in dairy factory farms. These cows spend their days either having milk pumped from their udders by milking machines or standing in indoor feeding stalls or crowded feedlots where they are often forced to stand or walk around in their own waste.

Lifespan of Cows

Cows can naturally live for over twenty years, but cows in the dairy industry only live an average of four or five years. These cows are not able to produce milk as efficiently after a few years because their bodies become tired and weak from constantly being pregnant or **lactating**. At that time they are sent to be slaughtered for meat. Many of these cows never make it to slaughter though because they end up dying from infections of their udders called **mastitis**.

Cows in crowded feedlot.

Natural Behavior of Cows

When cows' lives are not controlled by humans they prefer to roam open land, form lasting bonds with one another and forage for food. They also prefer to be in clean surroundings and to keep themselves clean as well.

Making Better Choices

Dairy product purchases have been decreasing each year as people are becoming aware of the fact that dairy is unnecessary to consume for proper nutrition. Almond, soy and other dairy alternatives are becoming more and more popular as people are choosing to take better care of their health and make better choices for the wellbeing of animals.

Forced Reproduction

It is a common misconception that female cows always produce milk and must be milked in order to stay healthy. The truth is the only way cows produce milk is by becoming pregnant. This is true for all species of mammals including humans. On dairy farms cows are forced to become pregnant by artificial insemination. After insemination calves develop inside their pregnant mothers for almost ten months before they are born.

Separated at Birth

The natural instinct for mother cows is to nurture their babies for many months and years after they are born. In most dairy farming processes calves are taken from their mothers less than one day after being born. This is done so that the milk being produced by the mother cow for her calf can then be pumped out of her and turned into dairy products to be sold. This happens several times in a dairy cow's life until they are either too sick or too weak to produce milk any longer. Then they are sent to be slaughtered for meat.

Newborn calf with its mother.

Calling for One Another

Mother cows are known to become aggressive in an attempt to protect their calves as they are taken from them. They also make loud and distressing sounds calling out to their calves after they are separated from them. The natural instinct of calves after they are born is to stay with their mothers for comfort, safety and nourishment. Calves make distressing sounds calling out to their mothers after they are taken from them.

THE VEAL INDUSTRY

Veal is the word for the flesh of young calves. In the dairy industry female calves eventually become dairy cows themselves, while male calves are sold into the veal industry. Veal farms operate by keeping calves in small crates which limit their ability to move around. Farmers do not want the calves moving too much because that will cause their muscles to grow. The more their muscles grow, the less tender their meat will be. Veal is preferred to be tender by people who eat it.

Intentional Starvation

Calves are intentionally fed a diet that does not provide them with the nutrients they need in order to be healthy. They are only given enough food to help produce the most desired type of meat. Due to the combination of weak muscles, poor nutrition and unsanitary living environments, these calves often become sick and struggle to even be able to walk. After just a few months the calves are sent to slaughter.

Calf on a veal farm.

Babies Want Their Mothers

Just as babies of other animal species need to be nurtured and cared for by their mothers after they are born, calves naturally desire this as well. Calves form strong bonds with their mothers after they are born when they are not prevented from doing so by humans.

THE BEEF INDUSTRY

Beef is the word used to describe the flesh of cows. Cows in the beef industry are farmed in order to produce various beef products. These cows spend the first year of their lives grazing on open land, often in very hot or cold temperatures and without shelter from harsh weather extremes. Once the cows reach a certain weight they are transported to feedlots where they continue to eat and grow until they are sent to slaughter. The feedlots are often cramped with many cows and dirty with waste from the animals. Cows in feedlots often become painfully bloated from being fed such an unnatural diet, and they commonly end up with infections due to their waste filled surroundings. Cows in the beef industry are usually sent for slaughter between two and three years of age.

Poked and Prodded

Before calves in the beef industry are sent out for grazing they are first made to undergo many painful procedures without medication to prevent or ease the pain. Countries have different regulations regarding these painful practices. Some places have banned the use of certain procedures, but they are all still very much widely used in the beef farming industry.

Painful Procedures

Disbudding: Horn buds are small nubs which eventually grow into horns. The common method for disbudding cows is to burn the horn buds of very young calves with a hot tool. The burn makes it impossible for horns to grow. The beef industry does this in order to prevent cows with horns from injuring other cows once they are sent to crowded feedlots.

Tail Docking: This is a procedure in which the tails of the animals are cut off to prevent injury of tails by other cows.

Ear Tagging: Ear tagging is done to cows in the beef and dairy industry as well as animals in other farming industries. A hole is made in the animal's ear using a sharp object. A tag is then placed in the ear which is used to identify and keep track of each animal.

Branding: Branding is a procedure which involves either burning or freezing an area of an animal's body in order to create a wound which will leave a permanent mark. This mark is used to identify ownership of the animals.

Castration: This procedure involves removal of the testicles. Castration is done to many male animals to prevent them from being able to reproduce with any females they come into contact with.

THE PORK INDUSTRY

Pork is the word used to describe the flesh of pigs. Pigs in the pork industry are farmed in order to produce various pork products.

Most pigs in the pig farming industry are raised inside of crowded factory farm buildings. Pigs can naturally live up to around twenty years, but pigs in the pork industry are slaughtered before they are one year old.

Painful Difficult Lives

In the pork industry pigs have their teeth painfully clipped to prevent them from biting each other. They also have their ears tagged, tails docked and are castrated all without medication to help with pain. Many pigs still injure each other because they become aggressive under such stressful circumstances. Such a large number of pigs are crowded together that they often have trouble even being able to move around. Pigs are forced to stand in their waste and often end up with infections because of their dirty surroundings. They are also forced to breathe in strong fumes which are in the air from all of the pig waste in an enclosed space without proper ventilation. This causes difficulty breathing and leads to lung infections and diseases for many pigs.

Smart and Affectionate

Pigs are naturally very affectionate with each other, and when cared for by kind humans they are affectionate with them too. Pigs have been shown to be extremely smart animals, even smarter than dogs. They also have very good memories and can even be taught to play video games!

The Sad Lives of Mother Pigs

Mother pigs are kept in small cages with cold hard floors for their whole lives. The cages are not big enough for them to be able to turn around or move much at all. The pigs are artificially inseminated in order to become pregnant. Once the piglets are born the mothers are separated from them by the bars of their cage. The mothers cannot care for their piglets in the way they naturally desire to. The piglets are only able to nurse through the cage bars until they are taken from the mother within a few weeks of being born. The mothers go through this experience multiple times in their lives before they are slaughtered. Mothers are forced to stand in their own waste which often leads them to becoming sick. They also form sores on their bodies from bumping against the cage bars. Many mother pigs die in their cages from infections or other illnesses. The rest are killed between three and four years old when they are no longer able to reproduce due to illness or exhaustion.

Unnatural Life

Mother pigs often exhibit abnormal behavior due to the unnatural and extremely stressful circumstances they are forced to endure. They frequently bite at the air and chew on the bars of their cages. Their **nesting** instincts are so strong that they often become highly anxious without the ability to build a nest for their piglets. They sometimes appear to build imaginary nests since they cannot build real ones.

Natural Pig Behavior

Pigs are naturally very social with one another, and when left to themselves in nature they stay together in close knit groups. They build comfortable grassy nests for themselves and their piglets which they keep clean and free from waste.

In cold weather pigs huddle together to keep themselves warm. In hot weather they roll in water or mud to keep themselves cool. They have strong instincts to use their great sense of smell to root around and forage for food. In the spring time they like to graze grass and clovers, and in the fall they forage for berries and nuts.

THE POULTRY INDUSTRY

Poultry is the word used to describe the flesh of **fowl** such as chickens and turkeys. Animals in the poultry industry are farmed in order to produce various poultry products. Most chickens and turkeys in the poultry industry are raised inside of crowded factory farm buildings. The massive, windowless sheds hold thousands of birds inside. The animals frequently become so frustrated because of the stressful environment that they peck at one another, sometimes causing injury and even death. Chickens can naturally live up to eight years and turkeys up to fifteen years. In the poultry industry they are slaughtered before they reach six months of age.

Turkeys and chickens are forced to live in their own waste which often causes infections. Fumes from the waste are extremely strong, and the animals have no choice but to breathe it in. They often end up with difficulty breathing as well as respiratory diseases and infections.

Poultry Factory Farms

In the poultry industry, babies are hatched in **incubators** and never have the chance to be with their mothers. Their beaks are cut off with a hot blade so they cannot peck each other in the crowded conditions they will spend their lives in. Due to the stressful living circumstances, many turkeys and chickens stop eating and starve within the first few weeks of life.

Against Nature

Most chickens and turkeys in the poultry industry have been **genetically modified** so they will grow much bigger and faster than they naturally would. Their abnormally large size causes many of them to become crippled under their own weight. Turkeys are naturally able to fly but in the farming industry their weight prevents them from being able to. Many chickens and turkeys are hardly able to walk once they have reached a certain size. Due to their unnatural growth they often suffer organ failure or heart attacks.

Natural Life

Chickens and turkeys are very smart animals. They naturally nurture and care for their babies for many months after they are born. They are very social and playful creatures and are protective of one another. Their instinct to forage and root for food is very strong. Turkeys and chickens also like to make nests for themselves. Wild turkeys are able to fly so they like to build their nests in trees.

THE EGG INDUSTRY

Chickens in the egg industry are farmed in order to produce eggs as a product to be sold. Most of these chickens spend their lives inside of crowded, dirty factory farm buildings. Some are kept in tiny cages alone or with other chickens, and others are kept inside of sheds crowded so close together they cannot even spread their wings. Chickens in egg farms have a large portion of their beaks cut off with a hot blade within hours or days after they are born. No painkillers are used for the procedure. The young chickens often have a hard time eating and drinking after their beaks are cut off, so many of them suffer from hunger and dehydration.

Living in Darkness

The chickens are fed much less than they need for weeks at a time because being in a state of starvation causes them to lay more eggs. They are also kept in total darkness for days or weeks at a time because it causes them to produce more eggs.

Chickens inside crowded factory farm.

Baby Boy Chickens

The male chicks cannot be used by the egg industry because only the females can produce eggs. Chicks which are hatched to become egg laying chickens must be female. Male chicks in the egg industry are killed since they cannot produce eggs.

Suffering

Many chickens in the egg industry die from infected wounds caused by other chickens. They also frequently die from diseases caused by the crowded, waste filled spaces they are in. The ones who do not die from infections or diseases are usually sent to slaughter by the time they are two years old because they are too sick to produce eggs any longer.

Chickens being transported to slaughter.

THE FISHING INDUSTRY

Fish and shellfish are used by the fishing industry in order to create products to be sold. Billions of fish and shellfish are caught and killed for food each year using commercial fishing methods or they are raised in aquafarms. Commercial fishing methods include huge nets or fishing lines with hundreds of lines feeding off the main one. These methods allow for catching hundreds or thousands of fish or shellfish in a short amount of time. Aquafarms are farms where fish and shellfish are raised in crowded, waste filled pools and tanks.

Commercial Fishing

Billions of sea life are taken from oceans each year. Many species of fish are in danger of becoming extinct because of commercial fishing. Scientist predict several species will soon be extinct due to overfishing along with pollution. **Bycatch** is also a common result of this industry. Bycatch refers to creatures captured by hooks or nets that were not intended to be caught. These include dolphins, whales, sharks, sea turtles, seals and many others. It is impossible for commercial fishers to sort through the massive amounts of sea life they catch. If something is caught on accident then it will die along with the rest of the creatures that were caught.

Aquafarms:

Aquafarms raise fish and shellfish inside of various water filled structures. Fish in aquafarms are produced artificially. This means **eggs** and **sperm** are squeezed out of fish and then combined so that new fish can be created.

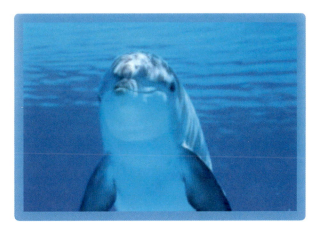

Scientists predict several species of dolphins will soon be extinct as a result of commercial fishing.

Natural Life

Aquatic creatures live very interesting and complex lives. They socialize and communicate with each other and can also be very playful. Their natural lives are much longer than when they are caught or raised in farms. For example, some tuna fish can live up to fifty years.

OTHER FARMED ANIMALS

So far you have learned about the animals most frequently farmed to produce food: cows, pigs, chickens and turkeys. There are many other animal farming practices which are not so well known about or discussed. Some of those farmed animals include sheep, ducks, geese, buffalo, goats, quail and bees. These animals all go through difficult situations much like the other animals already described.

Sheep and Lambs: Although sheep are commonly known to be farmed for their wool, they are in fact farmed for meat as well. Lambs, which are young sheep less than one year old, are especially preferred over older sheep for the meat that is obtained from them.

Goats

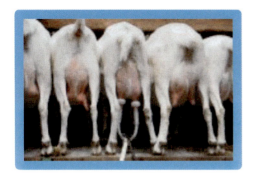

Goats are farmed for meat and milk.

Buffalo

Buffalo are farmed for meat and milk.

Ducks and Geese

Bees

Bees are farmed for honey.

Ducks and geese are farmed for meat and eggs. They are also farmed to produce a product called foie gras (fwa-gra). Foie gras is the name used to describe the liver of ducks or geese that have been fattened up by overfeeding and force feeding the animals. This farming practice and product is now illegal in many parts of the world.

Camels

Many people are surprised to find out Camels are farmed for milk. Camel milk is popular in many countries, not just the ones camels are native to.

THE HUMANE MYTH

Even in the nicest farming situations possible, most animals are still forced to go through painful procedures, unnatural groupings and habitats, and scary transport to ultimately have their lives cut short at slaughter. The word **humane** means to treat someone (human or animal) with compassion and sympathy. However well animals might be treated while alive, there is ultimately no sympathy or compassion in taking their lives.

Misleading Advertising

Words like free-range, cage-free and humane are used to advertise some animal products. These words often help people feel better about buying the products and make it seem like the animals might actually be living a good life. The truth is, companies are allowed to label products as cage-free or free-range even though most of the animals still suffer from being confined in dirty, crowded spaces, and forced to go through painful procedures such as having their beaks or tails cut off.

Farm Sanctuaries

The only farms truly as happy for animals as they can be are sanctuaries for rescued farm animals. These farms give animals the best most comfortable lives possible. They have space and freedom to roam outdoors, all the food and water they need to keep them satisfied and the companionship of other rescued animals and sanctuary workers who give them the love and affection they deserve. And of course farm sanctuary animals get to live out their lives as long as naturally possible because they will never be sent to slaughter.

ANIMALS IN THE ENTERTAINMENT INDUSTRY

Animals are used by humans for **entertainment** purposes in many ways. Using animals as entertainers removes them from their normal habitats and prevents them from being free to follow their natural instincts. Animals are often kept chained or confined in small cages or tanks when they are not performing or being trained. Animal entertainment industries often involve training techniques which are cruel and painful to the animals. Zoos, aquariums, horse racing, dog racing, circuses and rodeos are just some of the many ways in which animals are used for human entertainment.

There are countless ways for us to have fun and be entertained in our lives that do not require keeping animals captive and forcing them to entertain us.

Zoos and Aquariums

Many zoos and aquariums claim to exist to protect animals and educate the public. But most of them **exploit** animals, forcing them to live in **captivity** so people can pay money to look at them. Some zoos and aquariums do rescue animals and work to save **endangered species**, but most of the animals are either captured from the wild or **bred** in captivity for the purpose of public display, not protection.

Rodeos and Circuses

Animals used in rodeos and circuses are caused pain in order for them to perform better for audiences. They frequently suffer injuries and death as a result of what they are put through during training and performances.

Calf roping event at rodeo.

Greyhound and Horse Racing

Greyhound dogs used for racing are kept in cages for more than 20 hours each day. The cages are hardly big enough for the dogs to turn around. Thousands of dogs each year who are considered too slow to race are **euthanized**. Horses used in racing are often forced to run even if they are injured. Hundreds of racehorses are euthanized every year when they become too old or too sick to race anymore.

THE TEXTILE INDUSTRY

Textile is the word used to describe different types of fabrics which are made for the purpose of creating clothing, shoes, blankets and other products. Cows, sheep and foxes are the animals most frequently used to create various textiles. Rabbits, raccoons, seals, geese, minks and many other types of animals are either farmed, hunted or trapped so they can be slaughtered for their skin, fur, feathers or other body parts.

By choosing carefully which textile products we buy, we prevent the needless suffering and slaughter of animals in the textile industry.

Fur

Foxes, rabbits, minks and many other animals are farmed and slaughtered in order to produce fur products. The animals live short lives in tiny, dirty cages, and often suffer from infections and diseases because of their environment.

Rabbits in a fur farm.

Leather

Leather is the skin removed from animals so it can be used as a fabric for creating products. Cows, sheep, goats, kangaroos, alligators, ostriches, dogs, cats and many other animals are farmed so their skin can be turned into leather. They are forced to go through painful procedures and live in crowded, dirty spaces until they are sent to slaughter.

Down

Down is the soft feathers of ducks and geese. Ducks and geese are farmed in order for their feathers to be plucked and used to produce down filled products such as pillows, blankets and coats. These ducks and geese experience the painful plucking of their feathers many times in their lives before they are sent to slaughter when their skin becomes too damaged to produce feathers any longer.

Wool

Wool is the hair that grows on sheep. Sheep are farmed so their wool can be cut off and turned into various wool products. Sheep in the wool industry are forced to go through many painful procedures in order for their hair to be removed. They often suffer from infections and wounds before they are sent to slaughter.

ANIMALS AS PETS

People often love having pets in their homes, but unfortunately many pets end up in **animal shelters** or wandering around without a home or anyone to take care of them. Millions of animals, mostly dogs and cats, are **euthanized** each year because there is no way to care for all the ones that are continuously brought in to shelters. Most of the dogs, cats, fish, birds, snakes, hamsters, guinea pigs, rabbits, and other animals people like to have as pets, are purchased from pet shops or **animal breeders**.

Breeders

Animal breeders are people who **breed** animals in order to sell them. They control how often animals become pregnant in order to produce more of that type of animal. **Puppy mills** are an example of animal breeders controlling animal reproduction. In puppy mills, breeders cause dogs to become pregnant over and over again so that they are able to sell puppies to pet stores or to individual people. Farm animals, horses, cats, rabbits, hamsters, guinea pigs, birds and many other animals are also used for this purpose. Sadly many such places force the animals to live their lives in small, dirty, uncomfortable cages until they are too sick or worn out to be used for breeding any longer.

Pet Stores

Pet stores buy the animals they sell from breeders. This means that when anyone purchases an animal from a pet store, they are likely helping to support the breeding businesses who supply the animals to the pet stores.

Pet Adoption

There are always animals available at pet shelters as well as directly from people who can no longer care for their pets for one reason or another. This means that anytime someone would like to bring a new animal into their home to be part of their family, they will be able to find an animal in need of adoption. There is never a reason to buy animals from breeders or pet stores.

When we adopt animals in need of a home, we save them from the possibility of euthanasia, and we have the chance to give them the happy life they deserve.

ANIMAL TESTING

Millions of animals each year including monkeys, rabbits, cats, dogs, mice, rats and many others, are kept constantly in small cages and put through stressful painful procedures in order for products to be tested on them. Many of these animals are also used for research purposes either by researchers in laboratories or students and teachers in schools. The animals go through many tests and procedures during their lives as test subjects, until they are eventually euthanized.

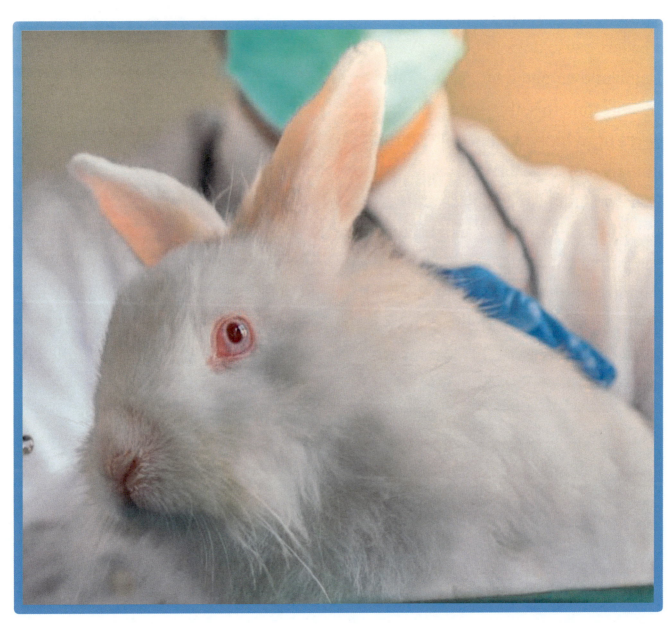

Product Testing

Some companies that sell products such as vitamins, makeup, lotion, soap, shampoo, laundry soap and other personal or household items, test their products or ingredients in their products on animals before making the products available for people to buy and use. They do this to find out if anything in the product might cause allergic reactions, pain or discomfort for anyone using the products. Animals used for product testing have chemicals and ingredients put on their skin and in their eyes, mouths and bodies, or are forced to breathe fumes into their lungs. These substances often cause burns, rashes, sores, breathing difficulty, pain, diseases, allergic reactions or death of the animals.

Research

Students in schools as well as researchers in laboratories use animals to learn about different subjects such as behavior, medicine and nutrition.

These animals are forced to experience many different types of stressful situations such as not being given food or water and not being able to be with their families or other companions.

Cruelty Free Products

There are ways to test products that do not involve using or harming animals in any way. Many companies care about the wellbeing of animals and so they choose not to test their products on them. These products are usually labeled as being **cruelty free** or vegan. When we choose to purchase cruelty free and vegan products, we are choosing to support companies who do not harm animals in order to test their products, instead of supporting companies who do.

CHOOSING COMPASSION

When we understand how much of an impact our life choices make on the lives and wellbeing of animals, it becomes natural to want to make choices that do not cause them to suffer. There are so many wonderful vegan products available now including food, clothing, makeup, body care, household and many other cruelty free products. There are endless ways to have fun and be entertained that do not involve places like zoos, circuses, aquatic parks or other places that harm or exploit animals. All of these options make it easy for us to make choices which include compassion for the lives of animals, while at the same time enjoying our own lives fully. Thank you for the compassionate choices you make in your life.

Check out the rest of the series!

If you enjoyed this book, be sure to check out the other two books in the Conscious Kids Series to learn about how our choices impact the wellbeing of our health as well as our planet.

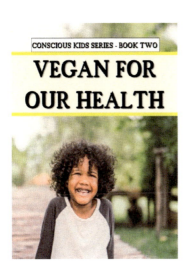 

Glossary

Animal Breeder

Someone who causes animals to become pregnant in order to produce more of them.

Animal Shelter

A place where lost or abandoned animals are kept.

Artificial Insemination

Sperm is taken from a male animal and put into a female animal to cause her to become pregnant.

Bycatch

Fish and other ocean creatures who are caught in nets or on fishing lines by mistake.

Branding

The process of burning or freezing the skin of an animal to leave a mark on their body to show what person or company they belong to.

Breed

Causing animals to become pregnant in order to produce more of them.

Calves

Baby cows.

Captivity

Being imprisoned or confined.

Castration

The removal of the reproductive organ of a male animal.

Compassion

A feeling of care and understanding for the wellbeing of others.

Consumers

People who purchase items.

Cruelty Free

Products made without using any part of an animal and without testing on animals.

Disbudding

Cutting or burning off of horn buds in young animals so horns will not be able to grow.

Down

The soft feathers of ducks and geese.

Ear Tagging

The process of making a hole in the ear of an animal so tags can be placed in them.

Eggs

The object that comes from female animals which is needed to combine with sperm (from males) in order to reproduce.

Endangered Species

A species of animals that is in danger of becoming extinct (no longer existing).

Entertainment

An activity or event that is meant to be enjoyed.

Euthanatize

To give medicine to unwanted animals which kills them.

Exploit

To treat someone unfairly by taking advantage of them.

Factory Farming

System of farming which includes keeping animals inside of crowded dirty spaces.

Feed Lots

A building or fenced in area where animals are kept so they can be fed.

Feeding Stalls

Small enclosed space for animals to stand in and eat.

Forage

Wander around in search for food.

Fowl

Birds including ducks, geese, turkeys, chickens, and many others.

Genetically Modified Animals

Animals that have been changed by scientists so they will grow and develop differently than they naturally do.

Grazing

Eating grass in fields.

Humane

Having or showing compassion.

Incubators

Device where eggs are kept at a certain temperature until they hatch.

Instincts

Natural urges and desires.

Lactating

Producing milk.

Leather

The skin of many types of animals which is used as a fabric for different types of products.

Mammals

Warm blooded animals which have hair, carry babies during pregnancy, and produce milk for their babies once they are born.

Mastitis

Pain and swelling of the udders caused by infection.

Nesting

The natural instinct pregnant mother animals have to create safe comfortable nests for their babies.

Production

The amount of products that are produced.

Puppy Mills

Dog breeding businesses which often mistreat the animals and care for them very poorly.

Reproduce/Reproduction

Animals creating more of their own kind by pregnancy and giving birth.

Sentient Beings

A living being who is able to sense or feel what is happening to them.

Slaughterhouse

A place where animals are slaughtered so they can be used to make food and other products.

Sperm

Cells that come from male animals which are needed to combine with eggs (from females) in order to reproduce.

Tail Docking

The removal (cutting off) of the tail of an animal.

Textile

Fabric which is used to create items. (Examples: clothes, shoes, purses, blankets.)

Veal is the name for the flesh of young calves.

Vegan

A person who does their best to avoid using any item or doing any activity which could somehow bring suffering or harm to animals.

Wool

The fine, soft, curly hair of sheep.

Made in United States
Orlando, FL
12 January 2022

13361027R00029